POLITICALLY
CORRECT PARABLES

OLITICALLY
CORRECT PARABLES

ROBERT MARTIN WALKER

HarperCollins*Publishers*

HarperCollins*Publishers*
77–85 Fulham Palace Road, London W6 8JB

First published in 1996 in the USA by Andrews and McMeel,
a Universal Press Syndicate Company, Kansas City

This edition first published in 1996 in Great Britain
by HarperCollins*Publishers*

1 3 5 7 9 10 8 6 4 2

A catalogue record for this book is
available from the British Library

000 628023 4

Printed and bound in Great Britain by
Woolnough Bookbinding Limited, Irthlingborough, Northamptonshire

For Brandon and Matthew
whose laughter brightens life.
Most of all,
for Donna,
beloved, companion, friend,
and unending source of joy.

For everything there is a season,
and a time for every matter under heaven…
a time to weep, and a time to laugh…

(Ecclesiastes 3:1,4*)*

CONTENTS

POLITICALLY
CORRECT PARABLES

INTRODUCTION

The parables of the New Testament are stories with a surprising twist. The rebellious son gets a party while the dutiful son sits outside and simmers. A laborer who works one hour is paid the same wages as one who toils all day in the hot sun. Ninety-nine sheep are put at risk in order to find a single lost sheep.

In a way, these parables are revolutionary. Conventional notions of good/evil, moral/immoral, righteous/unrighteous are pointedly challenged. In the mouth of Jesus, the parables are set against the primary form of first-century political correctness: Pharisaism.

This book is a satire of modern Pharisaism (political correctness taken to an extreme), not of the parables or the words of Jesus. The following stories are imaginative renderings of the original parables. Having profound reverence for these Divinely inspired gems of Truth, my intent is always to amuse and edify, never to offend.

When the "more enlightened" moral standards of our time are imposed on the parables, two things happen. The first is humor. The second is a recovery of the true purpose of the parables: to turn our world upside-down and inside-out.

What follows is humor with a purpose. In recasting the parables in politically correct language, I think you will see how absurd it is to impose our modern moral values upon them. The parables stand, as ever, wild and free of humyn efforts to tame them. Not only are they products of another culture, they are creations of Divine genius.

I hope you will relax and enjoy these stories. I like to think that after the original hearers of the parables gasped in surprise, sometimes they opened their mouths wide and laughed.

THE GENEROSITY-GIFTED
SAMARITAN

The Good Samaritan

Luke 10:25–37

ne day a morally righteous lawyer (admittedly an oxymoron) put Jesus' wisdom on trial.

"Teacher," he said. "What must I do to be eternally gifted with life?"

Jesus said to him, "You're legally abled. What does the law say?"

The lawyer answered humbly, "You shall love your Higher Power with body, mind, and soul and your neighbor as yourself." The lawyer was secretly pleased to display his knowledge of the law.

Then Jesus said, "You answered correctly. Do this and you will never be terminally inconvenienced."

But the lawyer, showing that he was not multiculturally sensitive, asked, "And who is my neighbor?"

Jesus told this story.

A male Jewish person was traveling from Jerusalem to Jericho on a road where he was likely to meet some morally different persons. In fact, he was soon physically abused by some potential clients of the penal system who invaded his personal space and relieved him of his money. Truly insensitive to his needs, they left him for dead lying beside the road. However, they should not be held responsible for their actions since they were economically and emotionally disadvantaged, having come from dysfunctional families.

A religiously inclined Jewish person happened to be traveling down the same road and saw the left-for-dead male Jewish person. Unfortunately, he was feeling-impoverished and walked to the other side of the road to avoid the medically needy person. A short time later another religiously advanced Jewish person walked down the road. He saw the medically needy Jewish person and, being emotionally impaired, walked by on the other side of the road.

Finally, a generosity-gifted Samaritan walked down that same road. Even though Samaritans were marginalized in that society and considered belief-impoverished by Jews, he stopped by the male Jewish person who, by this time, was severely life-impaired. When he saw the soon-to-expire person, he became compassion abled. He dressed the Jewish male's wounds and put him on his nonhumyn animal. He felt somewhat guilty about exploiting the donkey with the extra burden, but used an outcome-based evaluation to ease his mind.

The generosity-gifted Samaritan took the medically needy Jewish person to an inn and said to the inn-person, "This person needs medical attention. I didn't have time to take him to my Health Maintenance Organization. Please meet his needs and I'll make a transfer payment from my bank account to pay the bill."

Then Jesus asked the multiculturally impaired lawyer, "Which of the three persons was the most sensitive to the male Jewish person's needs?"

The lawyer unwittingly revealed his own moral dysfunction by commenting, "I wish I could have found that injured person myself and sued those morally different persons."

Jesus said, "You're not getting the point. Let me rephrase the question. Which of the three was a neighbor to the male Jewish person?"

The lawyer reluctantly answered, "The one who was generosity-gifted."

Jesus said, "Go and do likewise."

The lawyer immediately ran to the Jerusalem-to-Jericho road and began looking for victimized persons (potential clients) so he could enhance his income.

THE NEGATIVE-ATTENTION-GETTING SON

The Prodigal Son

Luke 15:11–32

here once was a father who had two sons. He also had a significant other who is not part of this story, but should be mentioned out of respect for equality among the sexes.

One day, the younger son, who was seeking self-fulfillment through independence, said to his father, "Father, give me my share of the inheritance that is due me."

In making this demand, the younger son displayed an entitlement mentality and showed disrespect toward his father. He was telling the father, in effect, "Since you don't have the courtesy to die now, I want my money anyway."

Now the father, being codependent, wanted very much to please his son. He gave his son the inheritance, justifying this by thinking, "Perhaps he will save the money, get a good job, and lead a morally responsible lifestyle." Of course, the father was deceiving himself, for his son did no such thing.

Instead, his son packed up his material possessions and traveled to a distant country, as far from his father's home as possible. There, he consorted with waged sex workers and other persons of questionable morals. To make matters worse, he became a negative saver. In other words, he greatly underachieved. This behavior, while self-defeating, was understandable since the son had been raised by a permissive father and an overprotective mother.

He soon ran out of money and was forced to get a job for the first time in his life, for his enabler was no longer present. Because there was a famine in that country, the only job he could find was as a companion of pigs. He was so hungry that he would have eaten the pods he fed the pigs, but refrained from doing so because they looked as if they had been irradiated.

One day he came to his senses, saying, "My father's waged workers have plenty to eat, but I am dying of hunger. I will go back and say to my father, 'Father, I have not lived to my fullest potential and am now economically disadvantaged. Treat me as one of your waged workers and I won't make any more financial demands on you.'"

The son rehearsed this speech over and over on his way home, until he had it memorized. When he turned down the road leading to his father's home, his father saw him. He had been watching that road ever since the son left, a symptom of his codependency.

The father ran out to meet the son. The son, expecting verbal and physical abuse, stopped and waited to be corrected. To his surprise, the father threw his arms around him in a bear hug and kissed him. The son, despite worries about the possibility of germ transmission, accepted these gestures as signs of affection.

The son began quoting the speech he had memorized, but the father cut him off midsentence. The father said to his enslaved workers, "Quickly, bring out my best designer robe and put it on my son. Then bring my college ring and put it on his finger and my broken-in sandals and put them on his feet. He will be treated not as a barefoot enslaved person, but as my offspring."

The son, stunned at this turn of events, wasn't sure what to make of this. It seemed to him as though he was being rewarded for his irresponsible behavior. However, he quickly repressed these feelings of ambivalence and gratefully accepted his father's inability to discipline him.

Then the father said to another enslaved person,

"Get the weight-challenged calf and murder it. Tonight we are going to enjoy the scorched carcass of a voiceless victim! What else can we do but celebrate? My son was nonliving and is now alive, he was dislocated and is now located!"

Now the chronologically advantaged son was in the field exploiting the land when the sounds of the party drifted out to him. As he walked toward the house, he thought it strange to hear sounds of music and dancing at three in the afternoon. He found an enslaved person standing outside the house and asked him what was going on.

He replied, "Your father has murdered the weight-challenged calf and thrown a party for your brother because he has returned safely."

Hearing this, the son became patience-impaired. He refused to go in to the party. Instead, he sulked and fumed like a pre-adult.

Then his father came out and pleaded with him to come in to the party. But the son answered, "Stop this rescuing behavior! For all these years I have been exploited like one of your enslaved persons. I have been obedient and morally responsible. Yet, you have never given me a scorched animal carcass so that I might party with my friends. But, when this negative-attention-getting son of yours comes home, after wasting your money on waged sex workers, you throw him a party! That's the most dysfunctional, codependent act I've ever heard of."

Then the father said to him, "I'm aware of my condition. I was victimized by a sobriety-deprived parent. I want you to know you will always be my morally responsible son. All that I have I share coequally with you. But, please, walk a mile in my sandals. I had to celebrate your brother's homecoming, for he was nonliving and is alive; he was dislocated and is now located."

The chronologically gifted son immediately made an appointment for his father with a therapist specializing in codependency.

THE CEREBRALLY
CHALLENGED BRIDESPERSONS

The Wise and Foolish Bridesmaids

Matthew 25:1–13

nce there were ten bridespersons who took their lamps and went to meet a bride and bridegroom for a wedding banquet. Five of the bridespersons were cerebrally challenged and five were endowed with higher-than-normal intelligence. This is not to make a negative judgment about the cerebrally challenged bridespersons, who were gifted with other abilities. For instance, they were very

good at stone throwing and other physically challenging pursuits.

When the cerebrally challenged bridespersons gathered their lamps, they forgot to take extra oil. The intellectually gifted bridespersons, however, took plenty of extra oil in case the bride and bridegroom were delayed. Of course, they were delayed and the bridespersons fell asleep in the banquet hall while waiting for them to arrive.

At midnight, they were awakened with a shout, "The bride and bridegroom are coming soon! Get ready to greet them with burning lamps!"

The ten bridespersons woke with a start and trimmed their lamps. However, the five cerebrally challenged wimmin found that all their oil had been used up while they were sleeping. Not having had the foresight to bring extra oil, they begged the five oil-laden womyn, "Please be sensitive to our needs and share some of your oil with us. Our lamps have burned out!"

But the intellectually endowed wimmin were not generosity-inclined. Instead, they believed in a doctrine of personal responsibility and adhered to the tenet of logical and natural consequences. Practicing tough love, they replied, "Sorry, sisters. If we give you our oil, there won't be enough for us. You had better run to the oil merchant and buy some for yourselves."

The cerebrally challenged bridespersons felt marginalized by their sisters' insensitivity, but were left with no choice except to leave and buy more oil. While they were gone, the bride and bridegroom arrived. The five remaining bridespersons led the wedding procession into the banquet hall, their lamps burning brightly. Many commented on the brilliance of their wicks, but withheld comments about the physical attractiveness of the bridespersons, lest they be accused of lookist behavior.

A few hours later, the other bridespersons returned from their oil-buying mission. They discovered that the door to the banquet hall was shut. They banged on the door saying, "Please, open to us. We had to get the oil merchant out of bed and it took longer than we thought."

But the bridegroom, who happened to be standing near the locked door, said, "Even though you are victims of nonlinear Eastern-style thinking, you should have brought enough oil in case I was delayed. Not only are you cerebrally challenged, you are foresight-impaired."

They screamed at the bridegroom, "Chauvinist, sexist swine! How dare you verbally abuse us! Marriage is domestic incarceration!"

In their anger, they doused the door with the oil from their lamps and set it ablaze. They then ran away, and organized an Oppressed Bridespersons Support Group based on twelve-step principles.

THE GEOGRAPHICALLY
DISLOCATED SHEEP

The Lost Sheep

Luke 15:1–7

nce several morally different persons gathered around Jesus to hear his teachings. Some were Palestinian revenue collectors, others were underachievers and non-goal oriented members of society. When the Pharisees and scribes, members of the cultural elite, saw these persons sharing Jesus' space, they said condescendingly, "This Jesus person welcomes ethically disoriented persons

and even eats nonorganic foods with them."

Jesus, hearing their classist grumbles, told them this parable.

Once there was a geographically disadvantaged sheep who wandered away from the herd in search of fresh grass. The shepherd, who did not exploit these nonhumyn animals, was the survivor of attention deficit disorder and took several hours to notice that one of the sheep under his care had become dislocated.

The shepherd was faced with a moral dilemma. Should he leave the ninety-nine sheep and go find the one dislocated sheep? If he did, the ninety-nine would have no protection from predators of nonhumyn animals. Or, even worse, an ethically challenged person might coopt the sheep for personal use. But, this shepherd was an animal rights activist who was committed to equal justice for all nonhumyn animals. So, he went in search of the geographically dislocated sheep.

When he found the sheep, he was exceedingly pleased. His self-esteem was greatly enhanced. He placed the sheep on his shoulders (he felt it would be too strenuous for the sheep to walk back on its own), carried it back, and reunited it with the herd. There was much happy bleating from the sheep that day.

Then the shepherd went home, called all his neighbors together, and announced, "Rejoice with me, for I have found my geographically dislocated sheep!"

One of his neighbors, who was emotionally different, said in a negative tone of voice, "You mean, you left ninety-nine sheep unprotected to find one single lost sheep?"

"That's right," replied the shepherd a little defensively.

"Well, I think that's a stupid choice," said the naysayer.

This person was immediately surrounded by the shepherd's neighbors, who were shocked at the negative and critical tone of voice he used. They immediately began his reeducation in how to be respectful of the feelings of other persons.

After Jesus finished this story, the Pharisees and scribes said, "So what are you getting at?"

Jesus said, "Here's the point: There is more joy in heaven over one morally different person who becomes reeducated than over ninety-nine self-righteous persons who don't think they need reeducation."

The Pharisees and scribes said to each other, "This Jesus fellow is the victim of nonlinear thought processes. He is spiritually dysfunctional."

THE HUMILITY-
IMPOVERISHED PHARISEE AND
THE MARGINALIZED PUBLICAN

The Pharisee and the Publican

Luke 18:9–14

ne day, Jesus was speaking to a large crowd on a hillside in Galilee. As was his custom, he taught the crowd using parables, because he respected his listeners' ability to think in an enlightened way.

However, he noticed that some of the morally righteous Pharisees had sneaked into the crowd and were whispering among themselves. They were pointing and laughing at some of the differently abled persons in the crowd and exhibiting judgmentalist behavior.

So Jesus told this parable.

Two male persons went up to the temple to pray to their Higher Power. One person was a humility-impoverished Pharisee and the other was a marginalized collector of federal revenue.

The Pharisee stood apart from the revenue collector, because he believed himself to be of a higher social class, and prayed, "Higher Power, I thank you that I am not like other persons: nonwaged, underhoused, morally different, non–goal oriented, or nonmonogamous. I am especially thankful that I'm not like this revenue collector, who surely tells untruths in order to economically exploit the underclass.

"I eat fat-free, sodium-free foods and lead a healthful lifestyle. I give 10 percent of my pretax income to empower the disadvantaged. In general, I'm a great guy. Of course, you already know that."

The federal revenue collector, standing at the edge of the temple, would not even lift up his eyes toward his Higher Power as the Pharisee had. Apparently, he suffered from low self-esteem. Instead, he looked down and prayed in a quiet voice, "Lord, please be merciful to me, an exploiter of the masses. I have taken advantage of persons who are differently abled, cerebrally challenged, and economically disadvantaged. I beg your forgiveness."

So that the Pharisees would get the point, Jesus commented on the parable. "I tell you truly, the marginalized revenue collector went to his home with the blessing of his Higher Power. For all who are humility-impoverished will be equalized and all who are humility-gifted will become self-actualized."

After hearing this, one Pharisee whispered to the others, "I believe this Jesus person has verbally abused us. He is definitely not right-thinking because he believes that a revenue collector's prayer could be superior to one of ours. He may be a Marxist." They walked away, shaking their heads in disgust.

THE ECONOMICALLY
ADVANTAGED, BUT
JUDGMENT-IMPAIRED, PERSON

The Rich Fool

Luke 12:13–20

ne sunny Palestine afternoon while Jesus was teaching, a difficult-to-please person interrupted him. "Teacher, tell my brother to divide his inheritance with me."

This person made such a demand upon Jesus because he was the chronologically challenged son and, therefore, entitled to one-third of the inheritance.

His chronologically advantaged brother had received a two-thirds share. What he really wanted was a fifty-fifty division because he was greed-gifted.

Jesus answered, "Fellow person, who do you think I am? A redistributor of wealth?"

The greed-gifted person replied in an abashed tone of voice, "I was expecting a little sympathy for my economic deprivation."

Jesus went on saying, "Be forewarned! Try to eradicate from your life all kinds of ethically disoriented behavior, especially greed. For one's self-esteem does not consist in the accumulation of capital."

Then Jesus told the crowd this parable.

There once was an economically advantaged male person who exploited the earth. Because he used organic farming methods, the land produced abundantly.

He thought to himself, "I can't believe I have been so economically empowered. It must be that I am specially abled in horticulture. But there's a problem;

I have created a surplus and I don't have enough storage space."

Being cerebrally gifted as well, he soon hit on a solution to his problem. "Eureka! I've got it! I will bulldoze my barns and build size-enhanced ones, even though it may mean compromising my wetlands and upsetting the ecological balance."

He felt somewhat guilty about destroying the wetlands, but justified the decision by telling himself, "I'll relocate the affected species to a wildlife preservation center." He was deceiving himself because he really had no such intention.

His greed became manifest, when he said to himself (for some reason, he liked to talk aloud to himself), "I will say to my Eternal Spirit, 'Eternal Spirit, you have accumulated enough surplus to last for years. Enjoy alternative relaxation techniques. Eat, drink, and make merry.'"

The Higher Power, who had been listening in, said, "You are judgment-impaired, and also differently logical. This very night you will become nonliving. And the surplus wealth you have accumulated, whose will it be?"

Besides being startled at having his private conversation interrupted by the Higher Power, the economically advantaged person was more than a little emotionally disturbed.

He shook his fist in the direction of the sky and said, "Who are you? Some kind of imperialist oppressor? I've increased my capital in a morally righteous way. I've used organic farming techniques. I was just kidding about destroying the wetlands. I'll acquire more land and build the new barns on it according to EPA standards. Doesn't the Higher Power have a sense of humor?"

The Higher Power answered, "Of course. I created the humyn race, didn't I? But you're still going to be terminally inconvenienced tonight. Everyone has to go sometime."

Jesus summed up this parable by commenting, "So it is with economically advantaged persons who accumulate wealth for themselves and upset the ecological balance."

THE FINANCIALLY EXPLOITATIVE PERSON AND THE ECONOMICALLY DISADVANTAGED PERSON

The Rich Man and Lazarus

Luke 16:19–31

Once there was an economically advantaged person who dressed in expensive clothing. He wore fine leathers made from the carcasses of nonhumyn animals and furs from cruelly murdered voiceless victims. He didn't care one bit that his fine clothing was tailored in Jerusalem sweatshops using pre-adult labor.

This person was a classic overachiever and an exploiter of the masses, having made a fortune in strip mining. He took egotistical pride in the fact that his wealth was gained at the expense of the underwaged.

He also feasted on cholesterol-gifted and fat-enhanced foods, caring nothing for his health. Every day, he dined on *haute cuisine* outside in his marbled courtyard while food-deprived persons looked on and salivated.

One of the persons watching was an economically disadvantaged person named Lazarus. He was marginalized not only by his lack of purchasing power (for he was indefinitely idled), but by incomplete health. From head to toe he was covered with herpeslike sores. Canine companions would come and lick these sores. Lazarus was so strength-challenged that he couldn't shoo the canine companions away, not that he would have harmed them.

Lazarus would have gladly feasted on the crumbs that fell from the economically advantaged person's table, even though such a practice would be considered unsanitary by the Surgeon Centurion.

It happened that both these persons expired on the same day. Lazarus became nonliving as a result of an infection he received from one of his sore-licking canine companions. The economically advantaged person suffered a myocardial infarction brought on by cholesterol-challenged arteries.

Lazarus was carried away by emissaries of the Higher Power and taken up to Heaven. As you might guess, the financial exploiter went to the opposite abode of the afterlife.

The exploiter was excessively heated in Hell. With flames licking at his feet, he became liquid-deprived and wistfully remembered the fine wines (with sulfites) that he enjoyed while alive. He looked up and saw Ancestor Abraham, who was sitting in Heaven with Lazarus next to him. Both were dining on heavenly foods similar to the cuisine the exploiter feasted on while alive. (Once you're nonliving, you no longer need to read the nutritional labels on foods or worry about fat and cholesterol content.)

The exploiter called out through parched lips, "Ancestor Abraham. Be mercy-abled toward me. Please allow Lazarus to dip the tip of his finger in his chilled chardonnay and cool my tongue. I am comfort-deprived down here."

But Abraham, who believed that justice eclipsed mercy in this particular case, said, "I can empathize with your situation. However, you must remember that, as a bourgeois, you enjoyed the benefits of economic power during your lifetime. You wore fine clothing and ate whatever tickled your fancy. Even worse, you ignored marginalized and differently abled persons like Lazarus.

"Lazarus, on the other hand, was a victim of societal neglect. He was underhoused, food-deprived, and involuntarily leisured. Now, he is empowered."

The exploiter cried out in anger, "What's wrong with this picture?! I, a productive member of society, am being eternally punished and Lazarus, a bum, is being rewarded!"

Abraham said, "There is no need for verbal abuse or insensitivity. The real reason I can't send Lazarus with some chilled wine for you is that there is a vast chasm between us that cannot be crossed."

"Why not?" the exploiter asked.

"I don't make up the rules governing the afterlife," Abraham said. "You'll have to ask the Higher Power."

"When can I speak to Him?" the exploiter pleaded.

"Probably never, since you just made an egregious gender *faux pas* by referring to the Higher Power in masculine terms! She has better things to do with Her time than listening to the whinings of a chauvinist like yourself."

The exploiter/chauvinist was much abashed as he said, "Please, Ancestor Abraham, send Lazarus to the male siblings in my nuclear family and warn them that the Higher Power is female."

Abraham said, "It's too late for that. Their social

conditioning has already biased them against thinking of the Divine as having feminine qualities. After all, you did come from a patriarchal society."

The exploiter made one final plea: "But if someone who is nonliving returns and tells them, they might at least become gender-neutral in their image of the Higher Power."

Abraham said sadly, "Gender-neutrality isn't good enough. They must be cured of their masculism if they are to have any hope."

THE EXPLOITER OF
MOTHER EARTH

The Sower

Matthew 13:1–23

ne morning, Jesus came out of the house he was staying in and sat down on the seashore. He was seeking some quality time alone because the crowds were continually violating his personal space. A person insensitive to Jesus' needs spotted him and spread the word that Jesus was sitting beside the sea. Crowds started gathering. Soon, the crowd was so large Jesus had to get into a boat so that

he wouldn't be pushed into the sea and drown. Since he had their attention, and they expected him to say something profound, he told them a parable.

There once was an exploiter of Mother Earth who went out to sow some seeds. Not being educated in modern horticultural techniques, he randomly scattered the seeds all over the soil. Some seeds fell on the hard path and birds came and began eating the seeds. Because he was speciesist, the exploiter began throwing rocks at the birds and they quickly flew back to their wildlife preserve. Other seeds fell on rocky soil. The rocks hadn't been removed because the exploiter was motivationally deficient. These seeds grew quickly, but, because the soil was shallow they were quickly scorched by the sun and died.

Still other seeds fell in the thorny wetlands. These lands were protected by the EPA and, therefore, could not be cleared of weeds. The seeds grew quickly there because the water table was high, but the weeds choked them.

Other seeds fell on rich soil, where crops had been regularly rotated. However, weeds grew more quickly than the grain and robbed one-third of the seeds of nutrients and sunlight. Then, phylloxera attacked another third of the growing seed and turned the crops brown. The last third of the growing seed was eaten by a swarm of locusts.

Discouraged with his incomplete success in planting, the exploiter hit upon what he believed was a brilliant idea. He sowed more seeds on the rich soil and immediately sprayed the area with herbicides, fungicides, and insecticides. As the seeds grew the problems that plagued the earlier crops disappeared. Some of the acres yielded a hundredfold, some sixty and some thirty.

However, it became known around the Organic Farmer's Market that the exploiter of the earth had used chemicals and people refused to buy his crops. He soon went broke and died from cancer caused by carcinogens in the chemicals.

After Jesus told this parable, the disciples got into the boat with him and rowed to the other side of the sea. Having Jesus alone to themselves, they asked him, "Why do you always speak in parables? We feel like cerebrally challenged persons because we don't understand their meaning."

Jesus said, "The reason I speak in parables is that seeing you do not perceive, and hearing you do not understand."

The disciples said, "What?"

Jesus said, "Because you obviously have special needs when it comes to understanding the simplest, most straightforward stories, I'll explain the parable of the exploiter of Mother Earth.

"The seed represents the word of cultural correctness. The hard path is persons with insensitive hearts. Whenever they hear the word, they reject it and it is snatched away by close-mindedness. The rocky soil is persons with limited attention spans, who receive the word joyfully at first. Then, after a short time, they lose interest and grow bored with it. The weed-infested wetlands represent persons who give lip service to cultural correctness, but then the allure of salary increases and promotions chokes their idealism and they become materialistic.

"But the seed sown on good soil is another matter. The good soil symbolizes persons who hear the word and internalize it. But, organic methods don't always work. When herbicides, fungicides, and pesticides are used, the soil yields abundantly. However, these poisons can kill you, as they did the exploiter of the earth in the parable."

The disciples asked, "Is this an explanation of the parable or a horticulture lesson?"

Jesus said, "Why are these mutually exclusive? You are victims of an outcome-based educational system. To those who are aurally challenged, let them hear."

THE DIFFERENTLY ABLED
ENSLAVED PERSONS

The Talents

Matthew 25:14–30

nce there was a male person, a capitalist member of the white power elite, who prepared to go on a long and exotic vacation. He called in his three most-abled enslaved persons and gave them his savings to invest until he returned.

He divided his capital among them, giving them unequal portions because they were differently abled.

To the enslaved person who was the most financially gifted, he gave five talents. (A talent was equivalent to fifteen years of wages for an exploited proletarian.) To the second enslaved person, who was less gifted but still a person of inherent value, he gave two talents. And to the third enslaved person, who was the least best at investing, he gave one talent.

The five-talent enslaved person immediately went to the Jerusalem Commodity Exchange and traded futures contracts on the carcasses of nonhumyn animals. Although he took much risk in doing this, the pork-belly market went wild and he doubled his investment.

The two-talent enslaved person was also risk-embracing. He went to the Jerusalem Commodity Exchange and traded futures contracts on metals recovered by raping Mother Earth. A mining disaster in Alexandria caused a gold shortage and the enslaved person's contracts soared. He also doubled his investment.

The one-talent enslaved person was not only differently abled, she was risk-averse. The fact that she was a womyn had nothing to do with this. Rather, her timidity was due to her suffering through a difficult childhood with parents who were negative savers. Therefore, she always acted in a way that she believed would lead to a minimum of financial risk. So, she took her talent and put it under her mattress, not even trusting an interest-bearing bank account insured by the FDIC. She reasoned that this would be the safest investment. After all, if she lost the talent she would have to work fifteen years to pay it back!

Several months later, the capitalist returned from his around-the-known-world vacation. He called in the enslaved persons to discover what rate of return they had earned on his capital.

The five-talent enslaved person came forward and said, "We made a killing in pork bellies. You gave me five talents. Here is five talents more."

The capitalist was ecstatic. "Well done, my financially abled and loyalty-gifted enslaved person! I'm promoting you. You will now have twice as much responsibility and a raise of three denarii a year."

The two-talent enslaved person came forward and said, "I invested your money in metals which yielded a 100 percent rate of return."

The capitalist was delighted. "Well done, enslaved person who is not-quite-as-financially-abled-as-the-five-talent-enslaved-person! You, too, shall receive a twofold increase in your duties, with a one-denarius-a-year raise."

Then the one-talent enslaved person came forward. Before the capitalist could ask about her rate of return, she blurted out, "Unlike your other two risk-embracing enslaved persons who were willing to bet the ranch, I invested your talent in a way that optimally protected your capital. You will be pleased to know that I did not put a single denarius at risk. Here is the one talent you originally gave me."

Now this enslaved person, who was expecting praise from the capitalist for her prudence, was unhappily surprised when she received the opposite.

"You motivationally deficient, nonproductive member of the underclass! You know that I am a capitalist and expect a higher-than-market rate of return on investments! At the minimum, you could have put the talent in an interest-bearing savings account!"

The enslaved person tearfully replied, "But I didn't lose your talent!"

"Are you mentally challenged as well? Haven't you heard of the concept of 'opportunity cost'? Take her talent and give it to the enslaved person who is now investing ten talents for me. As for this value-impoverished womyn, throw her out! She can see what it's like to be nonwaged."

The one-talent enslaved person wasn't as mentally challenged as the capitalist thought. She immediately went to the ACLU and filed a lawsuit against the capitalist for sexual harassment. She eventually won a settlement of eight talents and used part of the money to buy her freedom. She used the remaining talents, still a large sum, to set up a consulting practice specializing in helping risk-averse enslaved persons maximize their investment returns.

THE UNINTENTIONALLY SINGLE WOMYN AND THE INSENSITIVE JUDGE

The Widow and the Unjust Judge

Luke 18:1–8

ne day, as Jesus was teaching outside of Jerusalem, he noticed some discouraged expressions on the faces of the persons gathered around him. In order to encourage them to pray persistently and not lose heart, he told them a parable.

In a certain urban center there was a litigiously accomplished person who, naturally, became a judge. This judge had two character deficiencies that were especially challenging for those whose cases he presided over. First, he was respect-impoverished toward the Higher Power. Secondly, he was insensitive toward the needs of persons. This led him to issue some ethically suspect decisions. Of course, this judge was himself a survivor of parents with incomplete parenting skills. They unwittingly neglected him as a child while selfishly pursuing upwardly mobile career paths.

In that urban center there was a womyn who was maritally unencumbered. Her husband had become nonliving several years before. She, of course, was a self-sufficient person in her own right and capable of taking care of herself. She supported herself by working as an administrative assistant at the Hebrew Credit Union.

However, this womyn was suing her former employer for age discrimination. Her job had been terminated without notice, leaving her involuntarily leisured. She immediately suspected that ageism was the cause of her termination, even though the company claimed they were only restructuring the workforce and, therefore, had to downsize.

When her case came before the insensitive judge, he looked uninterested and dismissed it with a wave of his hand.

"I find no grounds for discrimination here," the judge barked.

But the womyn was persistence-gifted. She re-argued her case before the judge, claiming that she was terminated because she was chronologically advantaged. The judge again dismissed the case as a nuisance suit.

After this, the womyn became even more persistent. She pitched a tent outside the courthouse and called it "Injustice City." The newspapers sent reporters to cover her story. She became a local celebrity, appearing on talk shows and giving magazine interviews.

The judge said to himself, "Despite the fact that I am respect-impoverished toward the Higher Power and insensitive to persons' needs, if I don't rule in this womyn's favor, my reputation is going to be tarnished."

So when the womyn presented her case again (by this time she was in the courtroom weekly), he granted her real and punitive damages in the amount of several thousand denarii.

The womyn, now fame-enhanced, went on the lecture circuit and added many more denarii to her pension account.

A person from the crowd asked Jesus, "Are you saying that the Higher Power is analogous to an insensitive judge?"

Jesus said, "Of course not! I was using this parable to show that persistence is a character virtue when it comes to prayer."

The same person spoke up again, "You mean that the Higher Power doesn't hear our prayers unless we become pests?"

"No, no, no," Jesus said in exasperation. "What I'm saying is if an insensitive judge can be nagged into doing justice, how much more is the Higher Power willing to correct injustices with only a little goading."

The understanding-impaired person said, "Why didn't you just say this in the first place?"

Jesus thought to himself, "Persistence isn't always a virtue."

THE ETHICALLY
IMPAIRED STEWPERSON

The Unjust Steward

Luke 16:1–8

O nce there was an economically advantaged male person. He had a stewperson whom he placed in charge of his financial affairs. He gave the stewperson this responsibility not because he was himself incompetent, but because he wanted to enjoy elitist leisure pursuits such as polo, skeet shooting, and backgammon.

One day, a whistle-blower brought it to the economically advantaged person's attention that his stewperson was earning a less-than-profitable rate of return on his assets. The informer believed that the stewperson had suffered a judgment lapse and was skimming off some of the profits.

The economically advantaged person called the stewperson in and asked him about this charge, "What is this I hear about you not earning a reasonable profit on my businesses? I want you to conduct an internal audit and afterward you will be given a career-change opportunity."

The stewperson panicked, saying to himself, "What am I going to do now that my livelihood is being taken away from me? I am too strength-challenged to do manual labor and too pride-enhanced to accept public assistance."

He meditated on his future for several hours until he found enlightenment. The way out of his dilemma was suddenly revealed. Immediately, he began laying the foundation for future employment.

He contacted the economically advantaged person's debtors one by one. He first spoke with the olive oil vendor. "How much do you owe my employer?"

"One hundred liters of olive oil," he replied.

"Quickly, deliver fifty liters and we'll call it even," the stewperson said.

"You are truly generosity-gifted," the olive oil vendor said.

Then he called in the organic cereal manufacturer. "How much do you owe my employer?"

"A hundred bushels of wheat," the manufacturer replied.

"Just deliver eighty and I'll credit your account for the full hundred," the stewperson said.

"You're the kind of person I like to do business with," the manufacturer said with deep positive feelings toward his fellow humyn.

"You may soon get the opportunity," the stewperson said.

When the stewperson had given generous debt write-offs to all who owed the economically advantaged person anything, he presented his employer with the books.

"With just a quick glance at the ledger, I can see what you've been doing." The stewperson braced himself for the worst. "You gave deep discounts to my debtors. What a brilliant marketing strategy! I wondered why orders for my raw materials have increased twofold since yesterday. Forget about that involuntary termination joke I made a few days ago. I want you to keep your position here."

However, the ethically impaired manager had already received lucrative employment opportunities from several other companies. He turned them all down and set up a marketing consulting practice and became very economically advantaged.

THE NONRECIPROCATING
ENSLAVED PERSON

The Unforgiving Servant

Matthew 18:23–35

 matriarch was set-
tling accounts with her enslaved persons. She started
negotiating a repayment schedule with the enslaved
person who owed the most.

This enslaved person owed ten thousand talents, a
sum beyond imagining. How the matriarch had been
talked into lending a low-waged enslaved person such
an immense sum isn't part of this parable, but he must

have been persuasion-gifted. Of course, the enslaved person couldn't, in a thousand years, have paid back the debt.

Being somewhat unenlightened and also in a position to oppress enslaved persons, the matriarch ordered him to be sold, along with his spouse, children, and all their possessions. This would have retired only a fraction of the debt, but the matriarch reasoned, "At least this way I'll get something back on the loan. Also, it will be an example to other enslaved persons to not take on more debt than they can reasonably repay during their lifetime."

Hearing this decision, the enslaved person fell on his knees and begged, "O great matriarch, please be compassion-abled toward me. With time, I'll pay you back. I've already met with a financial advisor to consolidate my debts. I'll get a second job and encourage my coequal partner to resume her career now that the children are of school age. I'll make them get papyrus routes after school. Please, be patient with me. You'll get far more money this way than if you sell us."

The matriarch was suddenly seized by a rare emotion: guilt. She said to herself, "I have oppressed and marginalized this enslaved person by lending him too many talents. This is not economic justice. To sell him and his nuclear family would be exploitative." To ease her conscience, she ordered the enslaved person released and wrote off the debt.

The enslaved person danced out of the palace with great joy. On his way out, he happened to encounter a fellow enslaved person. He abusively grabbed his throat and demanded, "Pay me what you borrowed from me."

Now this second enslaved person owed him a hundred denarii, which was 1/450,000 of the debt that the matriarch had just forgiven him.

The second enslaved person, having only a few denarii to his name, begged, "Please be patient with me and I will repay you."

But the recently-debt-forgiven enslaved person would have none of this. He caused him to be a guest of the local institution for persons without assets until the loan was repaid.

Some other enslaved persons witnessed this exchange of ideas and ran to the matriarch with the story. Needless to say, the matriarch was patience-challenged. She ordered the enslaved person brought to her that very minute.

When he was before her, she said, "You are a very differently moral person. I forgave you a massive debt because you hooked my guilt feelings, but you wouldn't forgive your fellow enslaved person a minuscule amount. Not only are you nonreciprocating, you are developmentally challenged. Don't you think you should have been as mercy-abled toward your debtor as I was toward you?"

The enslaved person, realizing that he didn't have anything to lose, said, "You are talking like an imperialist oppressor. As a member of the power elite, you should be held accountable to a higher moral standard than a proletarian like myself."

The matriarch didn't buy the nonreciprocating enslaved person's argument. She believed in accountability and responsibility. Therefore, she said, "I will hold you to the same standard to which you held your fellow enslaved person. Take him away!" she ordered.

The enslaved person was made a guest of the local correctional institution and became a cell-mate of the enslaved person he caused to be sent there. The verbal and physical abuse they suffered there drew them closer together. They became good friends and coauthored a book condemning the matriarchy. From the book's royalties, they were able to pay off their debts and leave the correctional system as nonenslaved persons.

THE DIFFERENTLY
WAGED PERSONS

The Laborers in the Vineyard

Matthew 20:1–16

ne day at dawn, a vineyard owner went to the marketplace to hire migrant workers to pick grapes. These grapes, of course, were grown without the use of pesticides, fungicides, herbicides, or insecticides. In other words, they were cide-free.

After a short negotiating session, he agreed to pay the workers the usual daily wage: one denarius. They were happy to be working because of the seasonal nature of grape-picking. They went off to the vineyard and started work.

At nine o'clock, the owner went back to the market and saw some unhired workers standing around. He said to himself, "It is not good for these persons to be indefinitely idled. I'll offer them jobs, too." He hired them saying, "I'll pay you a fair wage, even though you won't be working a full day."

He did the same thing at noon and at three o'clock. These workers were all happy to be working, even if only for part of a day. In those unenlightened days, the only way to receive money was to work for it. As yet, there was no such thing as public assistance for involuntarily leisured persons.

At five o'clock, only one hour before quitting time, the vineyard owner went back to the marketplace. There were still a few persons milling about.

"Why do you stand here idle all day?" the owner asked.

"Are you sight-impaired or something?" one worker replied.

Another said, "We're here because nobody will hire us, even though we have taken an 'Aramaic as a Second Language' course. We're undocumented workers," they replied.

"Would you like to work in my vineyard?" he asked.

"There's only one hour left before sundown. It doesn't seem worth your while to hire us for such a short time," they said.

"I'm willing if you're willing," he replied.

"Give us a moment to talk it over," they said. They huddled and discussed the owner's offer of work. After much discussion they decided to go. Because of the time it took to reach a decision, they only worked for one-half of an hour before the vineyard whistle blew, ending the workday.

As the workers lined up to receive their wages, the owner said to the foreperson, "Line them up in reverse order of how long they worked, beginning with the ones hired at five o'clock."

When the workers who worked only one-half hour opened their pay envelopes, they jumped for joy. "We got an entire day's wages for only one-half hour's work! This owner is either logic-impaired or generosity-abled!"

Their celebration raised the expectations of the other workers. "Surely, we will receive a denarius an hour for our work, too!" they thought.

But when they opened their pay envelopes, everyone had received the same amount: one denarius. This especially galled those who worked from sunrise to sunset. They organized a delegation and approached the owner.

"We wish to lodge a grievance. You paid us the same as those who worked only one-half hour! Where's the economic justice in this?"

The owner calmly replied, "Where did you acquire this entitlement mentality? Didn't you agree to work for a denarius? I haven't done anything unfair. If I choose to pay those hired last the same, that's none of your business. Or, would you restrict my right to use my money in the way I see fit?"

But the workers complained, "If you want to throw away your money, why don't you throw some our way? What's equal isn't always fair!" They started to invade the owner's personal space by getting in his face.

The owner stood up and said, "Wait a minute! What do you know about fairness? Why do you think those workers were still standing around at five o'clock? They are differently abled with various physical challenges. Some are even chronologically advantaged. Some are undocumented residents. They almost never get hired. What I have instituted is a system of economic equality based on need rather than merit. I call it, 'the last will be first and the first will be last.'"

The disgruntled workers backed away from the owner, regrouped and held a meeting. They discussed the various possibilities for resolving their grievance with the owner, ranging from violent revolution to passive acceptance. Finally, they came to a consensus.

"We have carefully considered your 'last will be first' philosophy and have found merit in it. We will show up for work at five o'clock tomorrow afternoon. See you then."

The owner was rendered speechless by their clever manipulation of his system of economic equality. Unfortunately, he had no recourse, as he had no intention of picking the grapes himself.

THE ALTERNATIVELY COMMITTED GUESTS

The Great Supper

Matthew 22:1–14

 monarch, who happened to be male through no choice of his own, gave a wedding banquet in his son's honor.

When everything was ready, the monarch sent his enslaved persons to call those who had been invited. In those days, it took days to prepare the food. Therefore, the guests would be invited long before the banquet date and then be summoned when the dinner was ready to be served.

The guests refused to come. The monarch, being a persistent fellow, sent out another cadre of enslaved persons with these instructions: "Tell those guests: Look, I have sunk a lot of money into this dinner. I have cut short the life of many botanical companions to adorn the tables and have murdered numerous non-humyn animals for this feast. My chef has scorched their corpses to perfection. Either come and enjoy the banquet, or else ..."

When the monarch's messengers delivered the message, each guest began to make light of it. One said, "Silly monarch, doesn't he know that I'm a lacto-ovo-vegetarian?" He went back to his farm and harvested organic vegetables.

Another guest said, "Insensitive monarch. Doesn't he know about my commitment to an open democracy?" He went back to his job at the Palestinian Civil Liberties Union.

Likewise the other guests had antimonarchist leanings and mocked the invitation. A few were radical anarchists who mistreated the messengers to the extreme degree of actually rendering them nonliving.

When the monarch heard this news, he was enraged. He let loose his army on these guests and obliterated them and their city. He felt empowered by this action, not only because of the insensitive way they had treated his messengers, but because the food set out for the banquet was growing cold.

Rather than letting everything go to waste, he called his remaining enslaved persons together and said, "Everything is ready, but those invited had a change of plans and are unable to attend. Therefore, go into the streets of the city and invite everyone to the wedding banquet. This will be a multicultural feast!"

The enslaved persons did as he suggested and the great banquet hall was filled.

However, when the monarch made his grand entrance, he noticed a male person who was not attired properly for a wedding. This irked the monarch, who had provided wedding robes free of charge to the guests.

"Friend," he said in an unfriendly way, "How did you get in here without a wedding robe?"

The person replied, "I would have worn the robe you provided except that I have a moral problem with stealing wool from voiceless victims in order to make clothing. As you can see, I am wearing a cotton tunic not contaminated by any dye."

"It's very attractive. But you still need a wedding robe to be able to share in this feast," the monarch said politely.

"Could I just quickly fix myself a fruit plate to go?" the cotton-robed person asked.

This request sorely challenged the monarch's polite demeanor. He said to the wedding attendants, "Throw this differently-mannered person outside. There, he can weep and gnash his teeth while we feast! For many are called, but few are chosen."

The person was dragged from the wedding hall screaming, "Exploiter! Oppressor! You are espousing an elitist philosophy that undermines equality of humyns and nonhumyns! I refuse to shed one tear or gnash one tooth!"

Witnessing this display, the other guests left in solidarity with the person who was cast out. They staged a hunger strike to pressure the monarch into changing his robe policy. The monarch was left alone with mounds of rotting food and was fined by the Health Department.

THE TENANTS WITH
DIFFICULT-TO-MEET NEEDS

The Wicked Tenants

Mark 12:1–12

Once there was an exploiter of the land who desired to make wine for purely commercial purposes. Inspired by a profit motive, he cleared the land, planted a vineyard, put a fence around it, and made a wine press. He also built a watchtower, not to keep out thieves, but because he thought a picture of it would look nice on the label.

Being knowledge-deprived about wine making, he leased the vineyard to tenants and went abroad. The tenants made high-quality varietal wines, mostly chardonnays and a few cases of estate-grown cabernet sauvignon. Soon, Watchtower Wines were featured in all the best wine stores in Jerusalem and made a handsome profit for the tenants.

The vineyard owner, still abroad (it was an extended vacation), heard about the popularity of his wines and rightly assumed they were profitable. Therefore, he sent a representative to collect his share of the revenues.

The tenants felt that since they had done all of the work and provided all of the expertise to make Watchtower Wines, they were entitled to all of the profits. They were willing to pay the owner a reasonable lease rate, but were loath to share any profits. So they beat the owner's representative with vigor and sent him back with nothing.

Undaunted by the first representative's incomplete success, he sent another. He fared no better than the first. The tenants beat him about the head and shoulders and insulted him by calling into question his person-hood. The owner sent a third representative. Because the tenants wanted to send an unmistakable message to the owner, this one was returned in a body bag.

However, the owner was not gifted with knowing when to stop. He kept sending representatives and the tenants kept beating them or rendering them nonliving.

Finally, he ran out of representatives. The only person he could send, other than himself, was his male heir. He said to himself, "Surely, they will respect my son."

When the tenants discovered the identity of this latest representative, they were gleeful. Not at all understanding the nuances of inheritance law, they said to one another, "This is the owner's heir. If we murder him, then the vineyard will be ours."

So they seized the son, killed him, and threw him out of the vineyard.

Jesus said to those gathered around him, "What do you think the owner of the vineyard will do?"

When a person raised her hand to answer, Jesus said, "I'm asking a rhetorical question. The answer is that the owner will come with a host of mercenaries and destroy those tenants and lease the vineyard to others."

Those in the crowd nodded their heads in agreement and made murmurs of approval.

Jesus continued, "Haven't you read the scripture?

"The stone that the builders rejected
has become the cornerstone;
this was the Lord's doing,
and it is amazing in our eyes."

Then Jesus' point pierced the thick craniums of the Pharisees.

"Jesus is telling this parable against us! How insensitive of him to suck us into a good story and then turn it back on us. We ought to make him a guest of the local correctional facility."

But they were too afraid of the crowd surrounding Jesus, all of whom were roaring at the joke.